UNDERGLOOM

UNDERGLOOM

PRAGEETA SHARMA

FENCE BOOKS

ALBANY, NEW YORK

COVER IMAGES
Front, top: "Suitcase," Hedya Klein. 10 x 10 silk-screened print.

Front, bottom: "The Dazzle," Chitra Ganesh, 2006. 21 x 36 inches, digital print, edition of 5.

Back: "burning head," Hedya Klein. 10 x 10 silk-screened print.

Author photo by Katie Kane.

Front cover design by Aja Mujinga Sherrard.
Book design by Rebecca Wolff.

Published in the United States by Fence Books, Science Library, 320 University at Albany, 1400 Washington Avenue, Albany, NY 12222

WWW.FENCEPORTAL.ORG

Fence Books are printed in Canada by The Prolific Group and distributed by Small Press Distribution and Consortium Book Sales and Distribution.

Library of Congress Cataloguing in Publication Data
Sharma, Prageeta [1971-]
Undergloom/Prageeta Sharma

Library of Congress Control Number: 2013932323

ISBN 13: 978-1-934200-67-4

FIRST EDITION
10 9 8 7 6 5 4 3 2

Fence Books are published in partnership with the University at Albany and the New York State Writers Institute, and with help from the New York State Council on the Arts and the National Endowment for the Arts.

TOC

This book is for Joanna Klink & Rahna Reiko Rizzuto

In loving memory of Elvira Fraschetti

It is the word *pejorative* that hurts. —WALLACE STEVENS

ON WESTERN AVE

There is some drunk
song of contentment
from people who are not
day laborers, but
stand in the street.

And the Seattle gray cloud
of fret absolves mornings
of their quaintness.

I have slept well then I find
there's an insoluble dunk
my brain has toward the dark.
It finds the song appealing
but disengages its embrace.

I hallucinate wisps of steam
from the radiator as something terrorizing,
I must need to rethink how I'm seeing the stages
of contentment and what it looks like to invite grief.

There were loud noises outside my door
in the middle of the night;
and I attach it to a bleak narrative.
If my long thoughts require long bodies
then to formulate a formal feeling
is forever elusive and on top of me.

I NEEDED TO BE HAZY FOR A MOMENT

It's the only way to determine the grandeur.
Not for me—but for clarity in an all-purpose sense.
All ripe with the dullest intention—
let's all be hazy, unclear together,
a party for the apropos.
An awkward dance of dunces—
we act cavalier as a way to pass our time.
The experiment of living optimistically,
nonhierarchichally, quiet recluse of our outward self.
The malfunction turns cute.

NEUTRALITY MAKI

The outside is green, but let's pretend it's not.
Sweetened with vinegar the viscera will not apologize
for doublethink
nor for its neutral sheen.

And because of the sheer desire for certain principles not to exist,
Principle maki is never conjured.

Neutrality in its white edges,
torn placid sheet forgoes the innards—
A soldering ripe with ambivalent riches—
A clear sop of salty hipness.

The Somnambulist maki has more elation
because it is unexpected;
make sure your stature is line-right if your
gaze is eye-bright.

Your excuse—your disinterest—will be taste-based,
 the one who experiences an innate sense of primeness—
The one who experiences the lingam right off the phallus tree.

No place for my maki to rest—for I've learned—
holding a zero means you hold nothing.

Where is the neutrality in fueled splits?
Where discourse is false, and people falser still?

I have seen fits of pride,
lustration peeling down the drawn faces.

My science is of the edgy arrangement.
I realize it is cultural—and it struck me with its turn—
the false thralldom of terrible turns. Not a small
Geneva maki, not neutrality beside the sublime,
don't call it that—it hasn't been here.
It hasn't formed a face; it has fish for its brain
and the surface, only the surface, for a forthright simper.

EVERYBODY AT THE INSTITUTION

Until it is a foul mouth in the lobby of a stony, stipulated night,
nobody wants anything to do with insight and (doubly) nobody wants anything to do
with *recognizance*, and definitely nothing with *intent*, unless in the evaluation

Of outcomes.

She and I understand each other, clear of outcomes:
fever and winter are monosyllabic.

Men, too, are quiet in this town, they are awkward, dry patches of speech

with sudden, spare, desultory humor.

And others don't do a thing with empathy while blankets scratch pixels,
and mountains yearn for their sister cities, months dig bland holes.

People don't go near each other at the institution.

He cries and cries and is still deceitful; she, a fool, blindsided by her mop,
by her disinterest, but really by

her wish—if she could just have *this* one, she could be rid of all unpleasant obligations.

I thought I had this for lunch in another city; people wanting the same thing:
to lavish in the glory of double-occupancy.

I was wrong, it's not so simple, so
with my surreal-tip,

all that I could salvage, I wrote to find out if the people could come and go,

and they did, they were staging the poem for the conversation.

This is what we do at the institution.

It means our lives intoxicate only as symptoms,

how we compulsively squeal that everything *is* Michelangelo,

it can't go away, or the imperative would wash away with it.

DEAR POET

Are you the dark orange tree of night?
A persimmon ebullient in a cave of little thoughts?
I'm following your thoughts
and not another trend
in poetry.
But I can't be like you
because you are wrapped up in you,
in the purity of your *you* in orange.

THE OTHER PROFILED IN CERULEAN

for Eileen Myles

Could you look at me the way you look at him or her?

Would this mimicry allow for some kind simulacrum?

It would comfort me,

it would reassure me that I wasn't singled out.

I could feel comfortable.

I'm putting pressure on myself to write myself

into the narrative,

the word "myself," what do I mean; if I don't understand,

who will write me in? I'm only inside of reports and evaluations and things

from which I stick out; I think about when I and other brown and black people get

profiled in airports and in stores, on paper, professionals

or educators, portrayed as outsiders.

It makes me ill just thinking about it and when I write about it,

I'm not sure I'm doing anything new or revolutionary,

except just thinking out loud, on paper.

We have enough flattering verse: full of data.

I'm not sure how I enforce datum

in the poem except to explore its material sense on the page.

To place inside the poem the outside experiences—

not the ones where I am magnificent.

Too many poets love their magnificence. Perhaps

they claim words as objects for a kind of ownership of feeling.

This is what frightens me. I do it too. But I don't feel like it's always authentic.

FIVE QUESTIONS NOW STATEMENTS

The overused idea of "voice" gives me no useful

adjective for how to describe

the moment of powerlessness—of how the mind speaks in cries.

I am a sentence but not much more.

I am full of cunning and able functions, but not much more.

I am quantifying this smallness
that I admonish; but, somehow,

I then embrace
it in the abstract, as the Theory of Humility,
and hope it's concrete
enough to be much more,

and not the tyranny
of arrogance nor the troubling of the tiny.

GRATEFUL

Having the desire or reason to thank somebody.

Your poetry about outsiderness too outside the outlining norms—
it made you look ungrateful. Erosion of integrated feelings—
a breakdown of the soft side, like bad cheap bread—you could tell—
people thought they ordered a baguette, but they got you: bad cheap bread
dressed with bad dressings trying to taste good.

Of the towardness you yearn for as though it were inclusion:
Towardness replaced with something, not a
collective revolutionary subjective empathy. No descriptive abject space
to share with others—
the way you did in your urban environment,
the way you used to follow and share abject feelings with others
with a kind of careful and mindful allegiance (if this is even possible!).
And now you become the descriptive abject space and you're horrified.

On top of that, you find that everyone claims to be a Marxist
when really they're staunch constellations of teetering materialists—
so when you are a glaring materialist with inner Marxist tendencies,
you may appear tacky, but you are the outward of everyone's inward.
It's all the same. There are attempts to stick you with the bill,
to pat you with the so-so brush-off. Or, you think, everyone is a modernist—
flashing the collective rejection of individual heroes,
or limiting the play between subject and object to offerings of a specific alien play—
tending to the tiny, residual personal fires or shocks to the system.

However, you're no fool—you realized all this very young—
what t-shirt must you wear to convince them of this; a recess
for adults leads to more shameless bullying—an articulation
of disclusion, the patent expires on your wares;
you are interested in a new contemporary (musical) scene.

THERE IS AN ACHE SOMEWHERE IN MY BODY

It's a kind of treason to doubt the self.
You betray the body, planting so many obstacles to fury.
And to true so many ditrogonal angles, uneven and wrong,
to shelve the determinacy of a blank,
the burdensome obstacle, the unnecessary

shields that are always in place, it's a fallacy of spirit
of who you plan to be. *The body as a clock* is a cliché,
but if the body needs the clock to purpose itself, fit
with narrative, then so be it. Dyspeptic—
bodily pain, the unsway

of your lackadaisical shoulders, where's your heart's center?
Heavy, heavy loads, the brain frets until a thought
with substance intervenes: why, oh why? For him or her,
I care more deeply than myself? Why does this matter? Caught

in nuance, it's important to give some credence to
the languishing position of body—your agency is ticking.

CONTEMPORIES AND SNOBS

after Laura Riding Jackson

There's a structure for idiocy—lamplight—
all over the nation; it's an illumination
with such sheer creative force it is misrecognized genius.
I have misunderstood people's duplicitous ways—their lightbulbs—
as righteous forms of complexity;
not calculated obfuscations.
Much like the voice in a poem that insists it sing
the most important seer of light.
Am I providing this luxury as well?
Or is this my radical assertion in order to
call into question what an aesthetic authority looks like?
(That's my problem with the poem these days.)

(The light in my office flickers on and off—the lamp is broken.)
I see no enlightenment here, much like I see my acquaintances:
bright lights and night lights.
The fragility of the intellectual is the same as the poet's:
It's all about the *I* and its desperate sense of the *we*.

IN OUR SHARED RAGE

the clouds come over us.
We trouble the pallor of our modeled selves
our bodies are laced with filigree
our minds stuffed with dots.
We put in junk
to play with ornamentation,
we table psyches
with expensive trash.
Strangely, we feel liberated.

When we speak in fonts
that interrupt
with a size and shape and fury of flight
undoing the obedient decency
of our characters; then words dismount,
fables interrupting
byzantine spaces, variously garnished
with parenthetical sighs.
We, too, have misguided
and stylized largeness;
and thus feel ourselves
instruments quaking in turbulence.

Outcry can momentarily
harm the sphere of dialogue
breaking rhetorical semblances
with cultural interjections—this language has

accrued around us and when we
try these words on, sometimes there's pain.

But we don't disparage the truth, we call it erasure.

Hearts sing in troubled times; still salvageable to the ear
something that is not the lyric, a hoarse cough.
The ear *does* need a muscle, a drown dawn side-face,
a little village to pillage—away from sight,
a pardon from word-sounds, turns with logic and reason.

We noticed too many seated discuss our value,
turn away from others with a disgust
we discarded—that we put down.
Our paltry payment of blood
is for the foolhardy who find our faces menacing;
discussing them the way one discusses *fucking* and *copulation*.
Are these disgusting words?

Then there is newness in feelings;
there's aftermath in language now drowning in consequence.
It's a leveling, steel presence that somehow blinks and blinks.

WHAT HAPPENED AT THE SERVICE?

The forest service team came to my house to give me a thin-leafed tree,
and to say *you can have something, if you wish.*
You can have this native tree, a skinny branch, a skinny leaf
with bareness between the leaves.
A shrub like me? Here is my bark-being underneath.

The freight service team came to my office to give me a vermilion boxcar,
and to say *you can have something if you wish.*
Why is there no train service? No Amtrak? No russet cargo of folk,
no poets to embrace because our hands all unclasped in response
to the peptic ulcer of too much fanfare,
woods with austere engravings—plumed-pen-etched-words,
severe sentences with accusations— then interjections—
poets all alone floating skyward.

I have found the writing on the wall to be formidable—no patois,
no interesting resilience—I don't care for leaf rot
nor figures who do their own dance.
They find frozen ground menacing—they found me menacing—
even when they say in unison *you can have something, if you wish.*

It was not I who shoveled the shore and fixed it to another place.
I didn't find the pallor remarkable nor did I steal it.
I did however try to emulate it—pale-face looked feasible.
I thought I could have something but this was untrue.
I didn't take your sun.
I didn't take your eyes.

I've been trying to salvage the bitter roots that came my way,
the tincture inside watery and unctuous—
maybe the residue is sweet.
Or look to the river with its over-determined gurgles
in the vicinity,
small cascades immersed in scenery.

All will sound false to you but I can hear my real voice attempting speech—
but you happened to me—you ghosted your way through me,
you shrubbed me, not the other way around.
I know these things.
I have been down here, not up there—
I don't believe in powers that be,
but can see how the world looks up there.
How it knights itself with the grandiose: the majestic snow
of simulated faces, the whiteness that surrounds me,
and the quiet that follows.

WILD LIFE

A fostering of spirit and humanity dissolved.

This is the institution where poets are demonstrably immersed in their craft.

Words formed images in their insistence on seeing: "canyons," "ranges,"

and "valleys." Words formed particular insights into how within these landscapes,

birds and animals are seen, for example, the "Flammulated Owl,"

"Mountain Plover," or "Blue Sucker" emerge and confront the poet seeing.

These vantage points stocked with animals and birds induce

a kind of human throb—one that begets knowing how to see more deeply—

a rich, felt sensation. But what is seen in the poem about the natural world?

Perhaps there is a perception of some inscrutable invocation by a poet

with whom attributes under the scarlet sun unearth the stardom

of a creature of being, a form of other, sanctioned.

Who knew that in finding formulas one would awaken the insatiability

of the mouth eating its words?

The sheer velocity of certain kinds of poems with their orphic will

turning you into nothing, a poet as humble reader of occasion,

or you will find bullets and you will fire these words into the air.

What should I say to this kind of illicit behavior,

twindom turning to mob? Animals behaving like humans—

little sheep turn into diamond star wolves—a sharp shooter's mission to free fall.

The noiseless spider ate his own impure poem,

long legs breaking with need, and attention with the encumbered weight of snow.

HEY DAY

With meager spirit lodged heavy in the heart
I will notice now how it has suddenly turned abundant.
I am fond of particularizing in certain ways.
Exploring this thinking, in its sincere form,
as if it were a particular hey day in afterglow.
For example, last night we all hit the table with clenched fists
and the free-thinking—characterized in declarations
of expression tied up with the red string of feeling—
was so right in purpose. One attaches one's self to a person
who is an idea who in turn squeezes your hand to share it.

Don't discount lightness when it occurs, life with its usual
bare corrosive sense keeps abuse thick and present.
And so when we were all self-effacing in ways that felt spunky and kind—
I became elated, I was pushing my identity, the real one.
The one not struck with terror, the one not struck down by anyone.

This is what I want every day, what I want for myself and for the future.
Fumes of fallen rot go wayside for the hung, dissident tree-treasures.
I shake hands with everyone I meet—I say bring it on, I've had it all. Have you?
And now I'm justifying my means. I am not what you think,
I'm inside a world of smallness, of fortitude and sorrow—
it has all the trappings of symbolic engagements with society;
yet there is no poetry in people.

Moreover, I do love living for people in the way we must pass around the cup,
in the way we push ourselves in, through the door, with limbic certainty—
with challenged eyes and wires pulling us up.

WE HAVE TREES NOW

more so than we did before, but now we know what to do with them.
We hang our troubles on them and wipe our shoes against them.
We go lethargic on the porch, we tear the bark with spindly fingers.
We soak up the sun with restless hunger.
So much sky we say in unison, where does it go, do we follow it? Do we let it get away?
For months we splay without a fence, door wide open—
blue and brash inside and out. *Because we can*, we keep saying, *because we can.*
We face a lush sense of life that we have nothing to do with.
We face our cravings and journey with *a new kind, our new people*;
They all possess smiles and frowns, but more windswept
expressions—no permanent downwardness of spirit,
the way it was back east.
And since we've left the city to be ourselves,
we still must face our needy souls—
full of want, compulsions.
Were we proud of this? The way we turned away?

But we've protected these habits, forgone others in return.
What is the profession of the culture-hoarder?
Who are the gatekeepers? Do we grace them with our backs?
Moreover our chests remain empty yet seductively warmed,
burning by the fire, our asses cold and exposed.
All the wood, crisp birch to shield our lazy lobes, rounded bodies,
our cerebrums and other parts.
Are we awaiting cheerless ambivalence to greet us in the West?
Cavernous and cloudless, unaffected by beauty. Let's be petulant,
this is us now, we say. We can't help but find ourselves lustful;
crying alligator tears with pails to our eyes, *we didn't know we were here*

we kept saying, *we don't know how it happened*. We thought and thought,
and finally we closed our doors on the trees
to hide what we grew temperate for
but resolve didn't find us,
not alive with force, *we flew out of their arms.*

HALF-PROSAIC VERSE

We spent the year with two kinds of folly—
idiocy and madness—bustling from our storage bins.
It was in store for us, this new currency,
hazing to belong, to renew our own determinacy
of afterlife without the city.
A cultivation of the self
realigns the fabric;
the pleats have pulls.

To develop empathy and patience
like two-step for dunces;
to find a salvageable concept
in the word *experience*,

we must embrace how it's milky, how it's unformed, always.

The way we must be guided,
a brilliant moonlight that goes away

then six months of blindness and we must wait for it to reappear
as it has for others.

In the meantime we can point upward and make the gesture,
and we can decide if it is real.

Mind you, this is the kind of drama I want to preserve for the poem's
narrative, for its dénouement, because if it is here, then I could see
how it is constructed and defined, and maybe how things will end.

And, I *can* import the moon into my house.

So let me find it. And let me continue with the plurality of it all,
it provides me the kind of guardianship I need.

And to continue

We went to parties when there was no gloom.

We were heads bobbing about
with lettuce leaves sticking out our mouths.

We found that to valorize problems we must valorize their mission.
We gave them homely properties that they would become our own.

Events in sequence had qualities of tumult that eventually led
to ritualistic occurrences.
We personified them, made them into characterizations or behavioral impressions.
We took to people who were readily kind.

We sought white paper with edges like the collected arches of perpetualness.
We must learn how to organize the office.

There is the triumph of feeling over will, and the triumph
of will over feeling.

Each is miraculous,
clear and separate from the other.

Each is with the promise of contentment,
and when the year ends,
we will continually tuck
ourselves in for the coming year.

Each day was over and the next occurred.

Was it now the beginning of fire season?

The smoke was blank over the mountain.

A fine moment, when we bestrode heaven
and rode to the gravel pit.
I said to you, this was a damning experience,
first the family then the flood.
Then the flood to the disaster, then to the warm embrace
And sudden doom. We were here and we will stay here.

There was black blood and corruption, we filed
several complaints and knew defamation had occurred.
Was there a dark cloud rising up the mountain of conviction?
This was a daily fear.

I occupied a couch and searched
for information, I rushed against the wall.

Mist spread over our eyes, but we knew how to make it stop.

ADVERSITY

In this piggery you call prose is a state of make-believe
and one must see it clearly. You did imitate something real,
but it exemplified a kind of perjury of the self: malnutrition, bad will.
I could see it so clearly that I stepped away. You must ask yourself:
why do people hurt you? Opposite to a pheromone
is *exit crash*, your chemical substance.
You are not a member of a tribe of pastoral people for whom you speak
nor are you a martyr of developed fables.
I think this wicked rivalry of selves
does not speak to some engaging quality you see
in yourself—talent for being unusual, eccentric force of brain-will—
you are not the neem from a tropical tree. Your marching style
is a rucksack of illness. Pack your bags and find some pacificism,
it is a long road, with uncertain terms, and the mind that ghosts
so much will make difficulty insurmountable.

TRYING TO SPEAK TO YOU

after Kenneth Koch

I had a feeling that somehow we had irritated each other into a new space—
you wanted to remain you and I wanted to remain me.
So sad to keep silence with driving, a car engine and noisy radio pushing
against sound—both cantankerous: a screech chugging up hills,
different melodic wails. It seemed pleasant enough to try and talk to you.
The mountains in Idaho were already wasted on us.
But then I realized you were being antisocial and just wanted to listen to buried music
—you were digging it out. Music was more important,
the patterns had a terrific experiential quality.
I was getting in the way of what you were trying to listen to—
I was not paying attention to the needs of a sensitive person.
Sensitive people get over-stimulated prematurely, or prematurely in relation
to what we perceive as "normal," which I finally realized.
(My voice was disruptive to you.) And, relative to that binary
I can say that I am not so sensitive to delicate thresholds
in relation to stimuli. Something tiny with momentum made life bearable for you,
I was getting in the way of that. This could be torture for you. (I could be torturing you.)
I stumbled from the car, made a run for a mountain trail,
I think you felt relief inside, a slow, delicious creep.
I dusted the snow off my shoe, waited for an opaque swerve,
an eagle's drop, but a blighted mountain lion lost like me found me clear-headed
and engaging, we looked down at the cliffs of downward drops and ice for miles,
a car with people who chattered and gurgled picked me up—I told jokes for hours
and hours—this was how I finally lost all that uncomfortable silence and you found
that deep comfort rolling clouds downward, how it tempered you with its appropriateness—
a kind of implicit sound tunneling the rest of the world quiet.

THERE IS CLEAR DISCOMFORT IN EXPOSURE

Can we agree that it's something we all share?
Even if private vs. public is discussed.

Inscrutability is the only answer to power—
but to say I am inscrutable is to say what they always say;
the way shorn hair says everything about lack and space,
but can be hard to pull off without a menacing posture.

The way it's hard to mirror someone's shuffling and indecision.

Tether and sway
Tether and sway

It was the rope hanging in your performance that drew me to you.

MOBBING

The expanded gang started measuring me for stupidity,
with its magistrate, & I balked at this family with flowers. My barricade

was not for show and expressed shapely disagreement.
There are new words now for inscrutable: *not the right fit, not one of us—*

and it must be said that in mobbing—in blaming someone for all that's wrong—
the covered wagon of the West must remove its self-appointed fountain-pen,

bouncers, and punch-ups. For all that footwork is a suspicious performance carving foot-
paths only for the narrowest pedestrians: bully pencil-legs. Do not keep making

protégé after protégé for the conquest into dissolution. I, a coolie, admire the dislodger's
expediency & intrinsic disregard for the fumy other: her stink stank to you so you sunk her.

MY MOST BELOVED COMRADE TOOK HER LEAVE

What if I told you that I lived in a sphere
under too much scrutiny.

When that ended, silence
and when that ended, strife.
What was my weary task I asked myself.
Who here was the mother of heroes?

Valor and worth creditable, of course,
but in this remote city—
quite like a town—
I couldn't find anything but a forgotten helmet along a bike path.
When she was gone it was sad and I was so gloomy.

But she left me a javelin, which I threw quite far
landing me a cowardly lion who taught me
that there is indeed tenderness underneath, and that to find it
I had to undress my spirit of its purple sense.

THE WHITE FILTER

is peppered with a determined strain
bits of insignia that reflect
liberal musings with dropped articles;
careful references to the Great Masters,
but those masters will perform in lower case,
because they are more like friends than masters:
they are maestro-friends.

It's because the world feels like it's friendly enough all the time.

I mean that books belong to the hands that clasp them.
But what if the books themselves don't feel particularly thoughtful
or ready to be owned. Must we wait outside the premises?

I hope that even with my own
white filters I haven't sought to obliterate the kind of selfhood that I used

to admire: the kind that knew an abject state could reinforce one's personal
agency, the privilege of moving through spaces that were never given.

And now, upon reflection: Can I find a strain of selfhood that forgives
a bigot's poor upbringing but permits his certainty of my minority?
An ink that filters out the dust in my eyes,
enhances the glint of every wretched tome that uneasily dislocates
in its own wretchedness

but stands like a maestro-friend.

FOOL'S PURPOSE

For months terrible mannequins hung around.

I thought they were students missing words—
words they couldn't have—but this wasn't the case.
They had them, they hid them;
they even wore them when their clothes fell off.

Their stupor was a mystery.

Some of the language had gone south, into the undergloom,
it was where six of the words went;
they were my words, but they hadn't shown much promise.
Or at least that was how it felt.

I thought my colleagues had the words, but they, too, had missed them:
words that held important, wayward thoughts:
maybe misanthropic, disheartened, but mainly
those confused ones, salvageable, but no, inappropriate.

And you couldn't inscribe those in the classroom, so all fled—
I had wanted to keep them, but I forgot to write a memo.

I wanted those words that hung in the undergloom, stuck to the ferns,
the melodrama, the drop of blue with the hint of green.

Maybe a mission for the pauper:

I had become the pauper.

(It was either the pauper or the piper—I had been both.)

No music to lure; no brand new words.

I was the only one to say it was there, that it was part of the show

I had to sell the show
to get our narrative back.

And who am I to say this was all collective?
This is sheer arrogance.
The words, with their decorum, yet unknown to me.

I was going to have to go to the river,
I was going to have to learn to swim.

WILL YOU LET GO FOR RANSOM?

NO.

And so deep was the fall, what a drop; I had nicks on my knuckles.

A passage of time for all of it to hold you, then you hold it,
you wring it by its neck,
it's murderous and invisible—a darkling spot that grips.

And on some days, we would head to the bar. In the middle of the river,
the wail or the cries there found us.

Some colleagues shed tears from each eye.
Some other colleagues made them cry.

We tried handing them the words, but inaccuracy came fast.
I held my purse in my fist.

Was this a place I could get mugged?
I was reminded that it wasn't. I was still unsure.

I told you—
we are all like fish, happenstance,
troubled, out to the river and to the undergloom.

And glad I am, I took you in, and pushed the urchins out and off the deck.

I didn't have to tie you up—
you tied me up with several words, several serious words.

FOLLY STAMP

Clatter into the window this late night.
We were flabbergasted, tired
of the newly-minted drunks and meth-kids
with squeals for fists.

We live downtown,
exposed to the alley.

Nothing dangerous, and we were not alarmed.
But still, every sound turns us into pins on points,

a sleep of figuring out: deeply felt turns:
wrestling little autocrats

that fly or stick—nothing more than thistles
or wasps, but a sting is always a sting.

It must be we who are having the trouble:
it's our estranged perception of thinking.

Are we actually perceiving?
Do things truly mock us?
Or do we ourselves mock?

We must find our own modernization bill,
a folly stamp that appeases us with its generous
humanizing. We can be reckless, we can overreact.

Let's not be bewildered by the graces
that sometimes leave us,
by our paunches that are not always gargantuan,
that we haven't sewn shame in to suit our false selves.

The fit of relief or deferment is near.
What we find next is important.
What would happen if our window
arranged a life for us—
something intentionally
on view.

And we looked out at the reconciliation
of the rest of the world:
Wasps and drunks and meth-kids
arm in arm in arm in arm.

THE GALLOWS-BIRD

I don't think we bring out the best in each other.

I've said this to many of you and many
forms of you; but still, there is something
we could do to be more efficient in our
revealings, more sanguine
in our appreciation of and for our difficult selves.
When you complain to me about me
day in or day out, or analyze me for false causes,
I become irate: a hellebore, or a radical caricature
a hawk or hound with the bird inside the beak or mouth,
respectively. And am I poisonous or medicinal?

You tell me. So in becoming simply something else
to gawk at or to outline I see my shape.
I see my pencil lines are raw,
but my paperwork is not full
of white lines or loathsome studies.
Forthwax or forthwise, there are several
ways to grow into something formally
familiar. Find another galopin, find some other
errand boy, turn me loose to love the work
of work and the dignity of my responses.

PEOPLE ABSOLVE THEMSELVES AND EAT THEIR YOUNG

after Marianne Moore

The white light is hanging above the mountains, below it dusts us with cool air.

I am holding on to the notion that I belong here despite how it feels when I let go
of my thoughts and travel through my body. And it feels all animal,
        all a simple negation of belonging.

In the Katha Upanishad, "the horses, they say, are your senses," but in the West
there are horses and then there are horses. And to emote is to be defensive
        but one can be defensive if you have the right to defend.

        There is an ownership to the horse
and how its identity moves with yours, this is your horse-sense.

I tell people that I've been to Bozeman and I've met Turner's Arabians.
What does this now say about me?
I'm too fancy to understand plain horses.

Who are critics and who are believers?
Are they one? Do they force a tide? Do they string a fence?
        Do they find similes where there are none?
        This idea that your community communes is one I find specious—
this meaning is not fully delivered to me.

I'd rather stay out of it and tell you how Berryman sees it:
"it kissed us, soft, to cut our throats, this coast."

I stop reaching for live poets to guide nor do I find their horses;
I find dead ones who in their idiosyncratic ways return not to the horse,

but to their broken but functional feeders, their sturdy
hay, their world-in-general, no matter how fast it's moving

or how ignorant it is of its growing shadow.

THE TRANSITIONAL SERIES

Where do you study the turns of an ingenious device?
In an ugly room, one that makes me feel mischievous
and wedged in wooliness; the impact of a coolly controlled
force looking down on me. Another way to say it:
with Christmas lights and indecent responses to very decent exposure,
on my part. *What of it? What do you mean?*
Don't you mistrust ornamentation, too? It's optically formed,
it makes sure of a certain insatiable devotion with its performance
of itself clad in transgression, with a precarious diagram of positioning.
When is there no marker of the revolutionary space?
When I am in green flannel, touched by a kind of anointing
persuasion but I can't sustain it and don't know it.

PAN-AMERICAN

I should have been studying policies, but I felt shy
about my knees—I was knock-kneed and it
spread to my decision-making—each thought
was abnormally close to the last.
I became the person who buys merchandise
that no one would buy,
in order to be part of the job-share.
The products were maltreated by the popular ones.
There is a nice mock-heroic stance in here,
it's that I don't know any other way
and thus I can inadvertently become
a member of the mobilizing force,
a dynasty for which it is good to sway and bend.

HOGG VILLANELLE

for July Oskar Cole
after Samuel R. Delany

I certainly wouldn't want to watch. "Take my shoe off."
He pulled loose the top laces of the high, scuffed work shoe"
I crawled over, got my feet under me in a squat

His toenails were all picked way back too. I tell you it's about
as good as a blowjob any day. I licked them too.
I certainly wouldn't want to watch. "Take my shoe off."

Leaves slapped my face. Twigs caught my shirt. The sock
out the truck window. Hogg's blank, dumb look got through.
Piss had collected in the knees of my pants and ran down my leg, "You

Hargus . . . eh, Hogg? Hogg asked "What?"
No, no! Not watch of course not watch? We got work to do.
I certainly wouldn't want to watch. "Take my shoe off."

But I'm not gonna put my ass out for some crazy motherfucker like that
I glanced back at them. Between Hogg's legs I felt something move.
Piss had collected in the knees of my pants and ran down my leg. "You

Are parts of the letters, still wet, glistened. You are parts
that had dried to a dull rust. He vaulted up and through
I certainly wouldn't want to watch. "Take my shoe off."
Piss had collected in the knees of my pants and ran down my leg to you.

A SITUATION FOR MRS. BISWAS

When I received the call I was in a store in Missoula, Montana.

A store stocked with sparkling ephemera: glass fauna, tiny belfry bulbs,

winter white birch and stump-lamps brandishing light cones,

little shelves and branches hung with drops of ice and round silver baubles.

I loved the store: it was cavernous, dark with wood and burlap,

a ruddy brick loft with lithographs and monographs on birds or bracelets.

The store-owner, Fran, was away that day otherwise
I would have stayed in there a little longer.

She was a comforting friend—
she had impeccable taste, manifested in her put-together garments,
she also had a warming patient smile.

I didn't stay long, I didn't linger;
though linger is absolutely the wrong word,
more like I didn't stumble around there for hours.

(I would stumble around in that store for a full year.)

If she had been behind the counter I would have turned to her in
bewilderment.

∅

You see I had answered my ringing cell phone while browsing
(I usually keep it off in stores),

and my father said, *there's something I have to tell you.*
I don't want you to find out any other way. I am leaving my job.
They want me to resign.

Fran had met my father the week before—
he wanted to see downtown, the campus, get to know Montana—
he had done research on the education opportunities.

He was interested in outreach.

People all over met him and found him to be a kindhearted man.

I had set up meetings, he was here to meet educators, mathematicians—
more spirited people—I told him—than Bostonians.

I told him the West was a magical place. He agreed.

Later he would tell me that this was his last best day, a strange pun on the
Last Best Place.

Little did we know we would have to fight a very public battle.

And apparently from the rumors and from the strange
treatment he received prior to his termination,
there was a plot in place.

We, as a family, felt the public ridicule.

And as an Asian family, we felt the acute Asian shame. It was a dark,
disastrous cloud *hanging, hanging, hanging.*

My father would be publicly shamed
and we were shocked at the racist narratives—
allegations—a greedy brown man—

mismanaging, mismanaging, mismanaging

A public interest story to release venom—
to tease out *real* feelings from strangers.

Blog comments were aggressive: the Indian was a con,
a snake-oil man.

You just have to give them a scenario

they can invest in—in which to place those hard-to-place feelings.
White people bury their resentments beneath their liberalism.
 We *knew* he hadn't done anything wrong—we *knew* this was bogus.

Like I said, I was getting ready for the holidays,
I played hooky that Tuesday, excited to wrap gifts;
I wanted to decorate the house.

This was my first house.
My husband was out looking at Christmas trees.
Albeit I am a Hindu, trees are an awful lot of fun.

And this planning was quickly thwarted with the difficult—
my family was falling apart—
the droop in my life felt permanent.

I was more than 2,000 miles from my father, but his voice
becalmed me—
I felt anchored to his side—
I will stay there for as long as it takes.

Before this moment

I wanted to deck the table
with the kind of candles that beckoned, pulling you into an aesthetic presence
fully-fabricated and lit, and yet looked like it came from snow.

I had been in Missoula for many months,
I had come from Brooklyn, where I had lived for twelve years.
Now I was ready to escape.

Having been born and raised outside of Boston,
without the opportunities say someone like Robert Lowell had.

I knew I was not of that ilk nor was my father—we now realize.

Boston was indeed for the rich—with its stodgy colonial identity,
with its ridiculous Brahmins—
its oddly cultureless stance
even with Harvard as its mirror.
(Even with Cal front & center.)

Even so, I was pleased, I was unhurried in my new life, *I was, I was..*
I could feel how I stood, I could feel the rising happiness—of the belly, not the gut.

I was consumed with the bliss of poetry,
so much poetry around me, everything with poetry.

I said and understood, the workshop will be my ideology,
my intentional community, front and center—with bells.

My family was overjoyed with the way our lives
were working together—

my father was comfortable, my mother pleased,

a professorship and presidential position

at a college, he was the first South-Asian president.

He had come to America with very little and now had something.

You can see there is an immigrant narrative here.

When he first arrived, he made very little money as a visiting professor so he worked security at night at the Museum of Fine Arts. He kept thinking his colleague, Bruce, was calling him *bastard*, when he was calling him *buster*.

It took him months to realize this. He first had to confront Bruce.

The sequence of his first major purchases and acquisitions, over several months: a suitcase and a rug, then he found a dentist's chair for the living room.

He bought the Bob Dylan album that had "Blowin' in the Wind," because it really sounded Hindu—it sounded like it came from the Rig Veda.

For many years I would say he was a model minority—he aspired to being rewarded for his good work by white people.

We agreed, all was well— I had made my way to where I had wanted to be,

living a poet's life and it felt extraordinary—

all of the birch-stump lamps lighting up inside, this was a kind of bliss.

I had arrived where I loved in absolute terms.

Where I could love the poetics of if, then & thou. The luminous . . .

And yet poetry haunts with its suggestion that terrible things are true and stick, as Rilke says: *I am much too small in this world, yet not small enough/to be to you just object and thing/dark and smart.*

∅

The sun was hidden behind the darkest cloud.

I said what is happening to my father?

In response, my husband's back gave out,
he could not walk without whimpering, there was whimpering in the night

and I wasn't sure which one of us it was.

What was happening to my ableness?

We had failure, heaps of failure in our hands.

The world had recast itself in such a way that I had to address the power behind it.

I kept saying strange things to people like *no one is exempt from suffering.*
I felt like a tiny bird with sinking feet.

There are assertions about difference
That I had not wanted to make in the past, but now did.

Where was I? Who was I?

My father was told he had to watch his back
and then they took everything away from him.

To take away his dignity with so many untruths. Do I have to watch my
back too?

What did I think I could have? I wasn't even sure if I had it here.
People hadn't seen me as me, I started to feel it. Those glass birds

and the birch lamps were a kind of privilege
only others could have—not "others" in the sense in which I was other.

I started to see how money worked the room: when we had it, when we didn't.

Imagine, we were so close
to the soaring sky, and imagine how we fell.
How we knew falling wouldn't end us,

fall right here, fall right there, cry out, oh blustering self,
it can't be as bad as you think.

I said let's remember how to do it so it won't hurt
this time or the next.

But I had to say the branches extended their arms,
there was a house attached to them—

we found ourselves languishing, then needing
to rebuild.

It was the turning of the year and then another one.

And the showy, extravagant people capped themselves
on the tops of mountain ash—

we came out to clear them away.

WHAT WOULD NUCLEAR WINTER BE LIKE?

There are Wednesday moods
in tepid water. And, for example,
people in the word *everywhere*
that individuate the feeling of
comeliness. Like when I see a fawn
or a deer in these suburban regions,
lounging by a picnic table.
The whiteness of paint accentuates
tall pines in the distance.
Could all this be the same
when we find nobody
in the word *narrowness?*
And I can't help but think
it's the human being
thrashing its outer self
next to the trash can.
The plastic bags accentuate
some kind of inner horizon,
and rectangular hypervigilance
only frost and bombs can see.

THE WIDGET BOARD AND THE EARTH

In this sense my computer is my harvest and it sets up a dugout
for my beleaguered egotism. What I'd rather do instead of hunker down
in this no man's land is shine forth brilliantly; and, so, then, the effusive
style will allow me to franchise all concrete discourse that eludes me,
like a widget board through which Keats's "feeling about for its old couch
of space" will leave me not bereft of any invisible furniture nor with a concrease
of concussed feelings, but as a spiritual guide to the checkered violets growing
an overture over our black porch grave and our candy house full of moles.

POEM FOR LEIGH HUNT

I find ways to keep a sense of peace
but it is not always easy; for example,
I can't keep my questions tempered.
What kind of sun expounds its rays
upon the hills but then mutes
like an ordinary bulb, small
and self-contained?
Moreover, what moon filters
the blistering whiteness of
snow so that it can only enamor
the fiscally immune, the dully-noted?
Let me amble with Keats
and his wandering expression
and try to figure out if the poem keeps
me encased in a rapture for which
my dim external life won't account.

A BEFALLEN ELECTRIC HARP

If I'm not the most influential of the group
I still won't suffer the belief that my wide hearth
should rotate to its other side; a singular stop
will make my tumbler ache. I'm tired of the ache.
It's the pathetic bestowal, I want to say,
of the moon in its renewal, when it turns, when it speaks
only to me, cooing *you are my dearest child.*

I need this shape, it's a kind of pittance, its electricity,
even though the demands are dramatically
self-important, and not meager. Have some *Plaster of Paris.*
Everyone else, including the sun, says this.
Not the moon, though, not some Romantic fallacy
you can sing in haste, with your terrible personality
and that miserable space you say is the body of the poem.

GLENDA GLISTENS

Glenda glistens with a peptic sour
formed from hollow gladiolas
and wrench-shaped lilacs.
Why did they come for her?
It's because nobody—for miles—
can outperform her in self-mythologizing.

Lord Krishna himself fails:
he burdens the metaphor with his ungainly blueness.
But can anyone absorb the scale of her platitudes capsizing?
especially in foreign hands?
She can't be left alone like this:
without her harp, without her thistle,
without her myrtle tree's ignitions.

I fathom she will say that life's real heart-world
is too rich in hue for a trope.
She will have to transform yet another corpse's dander
and spin life's poisons
and spells into poetry's capricious
acquisitions.

POETRY ANONYMOUS

Do not fall in love with a poet
they are no more honest than a stockbroker.

(Do you have a stockbroker? If you do,
your poet is with you because you have one.)

If you think that poets are more sensitive because they care about language
pay attention to how they use language.
Are you included? Are you the "you"?

Or are you a suggestion?
Are you partially included as a suggestion?

> Are you partially excluded because you are a concept
> in some jewel-like nouns, almost throwaway,
> yet a perfect resemblance?

> How does narcissism
> assist you, who is also the object of desire?
> Do you enter as tour-de-force?

> Consider that this poem's vagueness doesn't account for your complexity
> and epithets don't suffice, you are not "one who is a horse-drawn carriage"
> nor are you a "sparrow with hatchet."

Perhaps they quote Mallarmé when taking you to bed,
carefully confusing you with their charm and faux-chastity.

All this before voracious body-pressing.
The lovemaking is confusing until, you remember, they said something:

thus spake the dreamboat, your poet, alarmingly announces during climax:

I spend my fires with the slender rank of prelate

and then fierce withdrawal with a rush of perseverance to flee.

You are mistaken if language furthers your devotion.
You are a fallen person now.
They care more about "you" than for you (you, the person you).

Line after line, a private, unmediated act done to you with confusing abandon,
flailing in its substance, however deceptive.

It will enhance your own directionlessness,
you will be harmed.

You cannot mediate it with caress.

Do you think because they understand what meaning looks like,
they have more meaning than others?
They are the protectors of feeling, mere protectors: earnest?

> No. They are protectors of the flawed,
> filling zones of bereftness.
> The aftermath of pleasure. A contested zone for all.

What about the lawyer who loves the law?
Isn't he just a poet with a larger book—

the way they protect and subject language
to sense-making?

A kind of cognitive patternization.

Ultimately, both undertake the hijacking of language,
they won't love you the way
you are; it's in this inability to love—
unless you embody the poem—
you embody the law and its turn of phrase.
Unless you see the poet clearly: loving utterance,
an unadulterated utterance—seized and insular.

You must entice with otherness.
         You must catch the poem as a muse does.
You must muse and muse and muse.

In thralldom to encounters that stand in for sexual ones,
we terrorize with sense-making,

it stands in for intimacy.

It stands in and suggests that all other kinds of feelings
and declarations yield to it.

It will move you if you ask for permission
to exist within its confines,

and you move the poet toward you and you hold the poet's head,
wrapping your arms around it

strapped in your wordless hold, but soon words do come

and in the trailing off of speech, you will be permanently lost.

POPULARITY IN POETRY

If A thinks that all poetry is this and that
B must believe A
To the exclusion of all else.

Scholarship and erudition
Prove this.

I recall Anselm saying all this popularity in poetry
Is for the young: *let them grow out of their batman suits.*

I DIDN'T SEE IT
for Adam

And I didn't see that now you were here on the page
writing poems too: poems silken with blue, fortified
with a metaphor passing through. But I knew this speaker
was you and knew there was so much about you that could reach
around the metaphor to a personal etymology, one that could brighten
and darken the poem without too many over-determined moves.
But if you, speaker, need figures—more than language— who bless
the poem's grief with vantage points or an altitude high
up, or bandages soaked in vinegar, sure, then let the speaker
invent a mirage, I understand that, too. It's tough these days when
anxiety speaks through the fission of thought; it's the piss-pot
of the mind. What anchors the fisted pronoun "we" in your poem?
Something must. And another thing, upon second read,
only now do I see how the "you" and "I" of someone else's poem
landed in yours: on that particular cited greenery.
And these other pronouns know—ahead of time—
to check the soles of their shoes and how to manage
a homonym's feet; moreover, they told you, speaker,
how to open and shut the door without too much invention
or conviction, which in a poem is rare.

MY OWN SUBJECTIVITY BOTHERS ME

for Brian Blanchfield

But yours is intoxicating with its modest, beneficent tone:
the remaking of yours to mine in nods of agreement.

Poetry is a fundraiser for the faux-haughty,
but also a trident for the humble.

This is an achievement.

Perhaps it's because there are always three ways to solve a problem
if prodded:

To flounder unbecomingly
To guess with adoration
To adorn, privately and publicly

The requirements make me confused
because the lack of detachment
to each is the new climax.
But that's only how to respond to one person—not several.
Duress for the appropriate equation makes a kind of thinking
subtract itself with no uncanny sphere.
We become diviners in principle where subjectivity is rueful;
our foregrounds mark our behavior and our cultural context.

Let's give in to self-praise.
Let's be stalwarts together.

POEM FOR MY FRIENDS

It's time for you to be the center of this page
because you got me through a lurid play.

The kind that makes you a pariah: richly outdated but not of antiquity,
a silvery shame, a problem coin that rattled for one full year.

Other friends have suffered too; we embrace each other, *not
falling in* is what we say, save for the moments

when frames were visible and entrapment did with us what it wanted.
We fish now, in our heads, with long wands of bait.

We tell everyone whom envy controls to stop planning the demise of others,
it will kill your own heartbeat too. It will. If we ever

talk about karma it's part of a specificity of the vertical address:
actions that are absorbed into the spatial interstice but are never untidy nor crystalline

and are never consumed by the self when it's trying to orient the benefactor.
Let the friend be something better than the benefactor.

EXHAUSTION FROM THOSE FORMS WITHIN
for Dale

It's the demand I make of you in times of trouble,
with unreflective turns and unheeded remarks.
Say we have our souls back, say we have more
than burnt bark. This last year, it was all about
the unkempt, involuntary motions—to sit upside the darkest day.
Except when we stole away, rich with extravagance:
wallets discarded on tile floors, sunk into deep springs
and hot water. Everything—we lost everything
including our collective identity.

There is a horror to the peripheral outside.
We nurse it and care for it—it's our tiny little portent.
And the working definition of freedom is to curl the nerves
away, to place an inscription inside—
a scroll of monastery inklings,
so we can record the silences and the trembles.

My heart is a disposable face,
a fleeting comedy—
a wretch that flies away, in trouble
with itself and not with you. I say this,
I write it in pieces all over the house.
More than numbers, we seek reasons,
infallible ones, ones
blood-soaked in status quo.

WHIRLWIND

Of the whirlwind that stripped it of branches—PERCY BYSSHE SHELLEY

Good are the whirlwinds that are true and just
and carry us away to an unreal—but are not mistaken
for illusory: not deprivation, nor have they abandoned the tree.
In fact they keep shaking the tree in play.
What about the moments in the poem
where things lay bare or bereft
or banishments are discerned
for the making of collapsible truths, and the poet
learns of this and determines it as a future?
And the whirlwind that passes by in *A Vision of the Sea*
and Shelley himself is still able to write
Death, Fear, Love, Beauty, are mixed in the atmosphere.
We trust this with a kind of knowable affection
and not other things? Here are those flashes outside the poem:
Humanity in the atmosphere,
in the form of people, their tenderness gained
where reciprocity is knowable and not actionable.

THE ROOM LIKE LIFE APPEARS FAR DEEPER WHEN IT'S DARK INSIDE

I was a story with nightmares before I was two stories with strobe lights;
however, lights when they dim without provocation sadden me
for they conjure up all of the feelings that promote waywardness.

Because I think I'm a strobe not a star, should I be a better
force of light? This is my problem: I find everything that's wrong
with me and set the table with *all of it* on display.

So you can see that there's NO ILLUMINATION TO BE FOUND.
I have to remind you that, yes, I was a beanpole before I was a pillow.
I don't know if there is a way to laugh it all off.

A pillow with its plushy demeanor and simpleton assessment;
a pillow for your bedroom of bedrooms.
Perhaps it's time to have a child: a baby who is my strobe light and my pillow.

I may need that joy, that sudden aberration where kindness meets the needful grasp.
But as I said the room appears far deeper than my need for it to stay like this—
and let me spend some time with it so I know how far I reach inside.

CHICKEN BEFORE CHIASM

And so, my life, where the ludicrous develops its sense of priority—
before anything else can happen. I see now that no poem appears for the faint of heart.

It's always the same: situations where fragility determines
the tempered verse: erudite or tiny?
O to be a genius where the lines roll out the red carpet.

It's the *Others* who did this to me. Did I tell you I was becoming one of them?

And during pivotal moments: when my love is roasting chicken downstairs,

and outside the baby wails for his tracksuit to feel less bunchy,
I am still here wanting to be the recipient of more human feelings

from other human beings. For now, a line will humble me
with decussation, wishbone chiasmus, I, poet of crossing. Hear

my willful chirp in a disgusted letter, *I*.

NOTES

Influences for *Undergloom* range from contemporary theory (Sianne Ngai's, Vijay Prashad's, and Homi Bhaba's) to themes of racial otherness in classic and contemporary prose (Toi Derricotte's *The Black Notebooks: An Interior Journey*; Langston Hughes's *The Big Sea*; Juliana Spahr's *The Transformations*) to the lyric in ancient (Catallus), Romantic, and modern poetry (Laura Riding Jackson, H. D.), and Peggy McIntosh's work on white privilege. The title and references to the concept of *undergloom* come from Part I of *The Iliad*, Homer (Fitzgerald translation); "Quarrel, Oath, and Promise": "Anger be now your song, immortal one, /Akhilleus' anger, doomed and ruinous, /that caused the Akhaians loss on bitter loss / and crowded brave souls into the undergloom." Much of the organization and writing of these poems was inspired after many readings of Helen Vendler's *On Extended Wings*, Wallace Stevens' poetry and other canonical verse—albeit distorted and paraphrased—that finds its way into some of the poems here.

ABOUT PARTICULAR POEMS

1) "We have Trees Now," "What Happened at the Service," and several other poems explore, figuratively, a kind of "bark" that carries a variety of associations inspired by Aimé Césaire's "It is no use painting the foot of the tree white, the strength of the bark cries out from beneath the paint."

2) The last line of "We Have Trees Now" comes from Bhanu Kapil: "They fly out of my arms. I fly out of their arms."

3) "Neutrality Maki" explores critic and poet Sianne Ngai's theories on cuteness, particularly: "Though a glamorous object must not have this mien at all (in fact, the meta-aspect of looking as if its aspect were subjectively imposed would immediately break the Schein of glamour), the subject's awareness, as she gazes at her little object, that she may be willfully imposing its cuteness upon it, is more likely to augment rather than detract from the aesthetic illusion, calling attention to an unusual degree of synonymy between objectification and cutification."

4) "Hogg Villanelle" All lines are taken from Samuel R. Delany's *Hogg*. This poem was written as part of an independent study with Montana graduate student July Cole, who proposed a reading of this difficult and important book.

ACKNOWLEDGMENTS

Versions of poems have appeared in the following literary journals, websites, and anthologies. I am grateful to the editors and poets who published them: *Academyofamericanpoets.org*; *Asian American Literary Review*; *Aufgabe*; *Boston Review* (web); *Disco Prairie*; *The Literary Review*; *Social Aid and Pleasure Club*; *Tight*; *Witness*: "*Adversity*" (reprinted in *Poetry Daily* (web)); *The HarperCollins Book of Modern English Poetry by Indians* (2012).

I am grateful, and can never be too grateful for what I have, especially for the support and friendship of Joanna Klink and Rahna Reiko Rizzuto, both of whom the book is dedicated to—as are some of the poems; and who are courageous—trustworthy inside and out—always spoke mindfully of the connection between writing and justice, and on true equanimity. I am grateful to Katy Lederer, a friend who lifts me up practically, soulfully, and with an earned wisdom that guides, and to Katie Kane, Ken White, and Louise Economides for your kindness, acumen, and care. Thanks for the extraordinary artistic gifts of Chitra Ganesh and Hedya Klein; I appreciate your sharing these powerful images with me. Thank you Rebecca Wolff for your brilliance as a writer, editor, publisher, and friend; you have helped me so much. Thank you to Brian Blanchfield, Deb Busch and Patrick Hutchins, Bridget Carson and Christina "Spidey" McKnight, Casey Charles, Elizabeth Robinson, Angelica Lawson and Clint Carroll, Eileen Myles, Lee Heuermann, Lisa Jarrett and Burke Jam, Peter Orner, Kate Shanley and David Moore, Lynn Itagaki and Devin Fergus, Danzy

Senna, Peter Richards and Bindu Panikkar, Nancy Cook, Andrew Smith and Courtney Saunders—all a particular soulful Missoula (& elsewhere) posse. Thank you to the Naropa community, Goddard colleagues, Dorothy Wang, and Magdalena Zurawski. Thank you to UM graduate and undergraduate students for your support and feedback to my poems and teaching; I enjoy learning from you. Thank you to Jocelyn Siler and Gerald Fetz. Thank you to the Howard Foundation (thank you Elizabeth Willis), University of Montana English Dept., to Peter Baker, Mehrdad Kia, and to the UMT Faculty Development Grant. Thank you also to Kundiman, Hotel Pupik, The Millay Colony, and Headlands Center for the Arts; ideas, revisions, writing happened with your support. Thank you to Emery Jones and Elizabeth O'Halloran.

Words are not enough to thank my loving parents, Bimla and Mahesh Sharma, whose strength is awe-inducing; power, mighty; understanding of resilience, sharply perceptive. Thank you, Manu. My dear husband Dale Sherrard, who stayed strong even when he felt things go. You are deeply loved. Thank you to Aja Mujinga Sherrard for our ongoing, rich conversations about family, race, and identity.

Borrowing an already borrowed quotation of Paulo Freire from Bell Hooks's *Belonging: On Place*: "Suffering exile implies recognizing that one has left his or her context of origin: it means experiencing bitterness, the clarity of a cloudy place where one must make right moves to get through. Exile cannot be suffered when it is all pain and pessimism. Exile cannot be suffered when it is all reason. One suffers exile when his or her conscious body, reason, and feeling—one's whole body—is touched . . . To have a project for the future, I do not live only in the past. Rather, I exist in the present, where I prepare myself for the possible return."

C

FENCE BOOKS

OTTOLINE PRIZE
Inter Arma   Lauren Shufran

MOTHERWELL & ALBERTA PRIZE
Negro League Baseball	Harmony Holiday
living must bury	Josie Sigler
Aim Straight at the Fountain and Press Vaporize	Elizabeth Marie Young
Unspoiled Air	Kaisa Ullsvik Miller
The Cow	Ariana Reines
Practice, Restraint	Laura Sims
A Magic Book	Sasha Steensen
Sky Girl	Rosemary Griggs
The Real Moon of Poetry and Other Poems	Tina Brown Celona
Zirconia	Chelsey Minnis

FENCE MODERN POETS SERIES
In the Laurels, Caught	Lee Ann Brown
Eyelid Lick	Donald Dunbar
Nick Demske	Nick Demske
Duties of an English Foreign Secretary	Macgregor Card
Star in the Eye	James Shea
Structure of the Embryonic Rat Brain	Christopher Janke
The Stupefying Flashbulbs	Daniel Brenner
Povel	Geraldine Kim
The Opening Question	Prageeta Sharma
Apprehend	Elizabeth Robinson
The Red Bird	Joyelle McSweeney

NATIONAL POETRY SERIES
Your Invitation to a Modest Breakfast	Hannah Gamble
A Map Predetermined and Chance	Laura Wetherington
The Network	Jena Osman
The Black Automaton	Douglas Kearney
Collapsible Poetics Theater	Rodrigo Toscano

ANTHOLOGIES & CRITICAL WORKS
Not for Mothers Only: Contemporary Poets on Child-Getting & Child-Rearing
            Catherine Wagner & Rebecca Wolff, editors
A Best of Fence: *The First Nine Years*, Volumes 1 & 2
            Rebecca Wolff and Fence Editors, editors

POETRY

A Book Beginning What and Ending Away	Clark Coolidge
88 Sonnets	Clark Coolidge
Mellow Actions	Brandon Downing
Percussion Grenade	Joyelle McSweeney
Coeur de Lion	Ariana Reines
June	Daniel Brenner
English Fragments A Brief History of the Soul	Martin Corless-Smith
The Sore Throat & Other Poems	Aaron Kunin
Dead Ahead	Ben Doller
My New Job	Catherine Wagner
Stranger	Laura Sims
The Method	Sasha Steensen
The Orphan & Its Relations	Elizabeth Robinson
Site Acquisition	Brian Young
Rogue Hemlocks	Carl Martin
19 Names for Our Band	Jibade-Khalil Huffman
Infamous Landscapes	Prageeta Sharma
Bad Bad	Chelsey Minnis
Snip Snip!	Tina Brown Celona
Yes, Master	Michael Earl Craig
Swallows	Martin Corless-Smith
Folding Ruler Star	Aaron Kunin
The Commandrine & Other Poems	Joyelle McSweeney
Macular Hole	Catherine Wagner
Nota	Martin Corless-Smith
Father of Noise	Anthony McCann
Can You Relax in My House	Michael Earl Craig
Miss America	Catherine Wagner

FICTION

Prayer and Parable: Stories	Paul Maliszewski
Flet: A Novel	Joyelle McSweeney
The Mandarin	Aaron Kunin